BODY LANGUAGE

UNDERSTANDING BODY LANGUAGE IN UNDER AN HOUR

Analyzing People, Reading Minds, Brain Physiology

Dr. Christopher Nash

TABLE OF CONTENTS

INTRODUCTION

It's in the natural order of things to "size up" a person within the first few seconds of the first meeting between two people. We all do it subconsciously and despite our best efforts to reserve judgment until we have all the facts, we cannot fight the urge to create a profile and then wait or try to prove or disprove the facts that we put in that profile after those first few seconds. It would be useless to try and deny that we do it. In fact there are some people that take pride in doing it and then gossip about their observations without real evidence to back up their claims.

Some people have a natural charisma to read someone right from the start and be right about it. Some others fall into the mistake of creating a profile and then refuse to change it when the facts contradict the initial judgment. Most of us can adapt to the facts about a person's personality that result after the observation of that person's actions and behavioral patterns.

The whole idea behind the contents of this book is to incorporate some knowledge and some proven facts in this process that can help us make this initial judgment and sizing up as solid as possible. The natural process is based solely on instinct and experience. If a few rules can be added to broaden the spectrum of the initial analysis then in most likelihood we will be able to analyze a person right from the start and mostly be correct about it.

The way someone talks, the way the phrases are articulated, the vocabulary used, the way he or she is dressed, the total sum of the way a person is "set up", even the way they walk, are indications of who they are. All the above belong to concepts like "verbal", "paraverbal" and "non-verbal" communication (what we used to know as body language) that will be explored in this book.

There is no use in trying to deny that all the above are facts and that the advice that is always given to people not to judge anyone after just a few seconds is not adhered to in 99,99% of the cases. Which makes it necessary to make this process as knowledgeable and as thorough as possible by learning what to look for and how to interpret the signals we receive. Actually this last part is most important.

These signals are always sent and it takes years of training to masque them. Trying to cover them, either for professional or for personal reasons, is a sign that we either have something to hide or that we are dishonest to begin with. For a seasoned observer the covering process is always obvious as it leaves a feeling of improvisation. It also leaves distinct marks that there has been training involved. We will also be discussing a few ways that this kind of covering can be detected and how it is possible to cut through the deception and see what lies behind.

The bottom line of the exercise is to acquire the ability to make the initial analysis as precise and as correct as possible to avoid making mistakes in the process of a relationship with a person. The term is not used to describe a personal relationship. It is used to describe any sort of interaction between two people. From a simple acquaintance to a complex professional cooperation.

Being wrong in an acquaintance may not be anything more than an annoyance. A complex relationship on the other hand may include the possibility of losing a lot more than just money. According to the psychologists a great number of suicides could have been prevented if the people could have been shown the way to correctly assess what they were getting themselves into.

This is how important learning to correctly size up a person can be. It is not a professional way and it is not infallible. But it will save people a lot of hardship if they can know about a few things in advance and protect themselves accordingly.

THE FIRST IMPRESSION

How many of us have exclaimed "What a (insert your own characterization here)!" after having seen a person for the first time? How many have turned away from a person poorly dressed, dirty and with a long beard? How many have grimaced in disgust at the sight of a person (especially women) that presents themselves with what we consider as a poor taste in style? And how many have just turned away from any kind of relationship with such persons? Has any of you ever wondered that you may have been wrong in these assumptions?

If anyone would take a first glance at a person looking like Einstein without the proper context in his or her analysis, would simply turn away based on all the above. The photos of Einstein's long hair and poor sense of style for the era are world famous. Yet, we are talking about one of the greatest minds that ever walked on the surface of this planet!

First impressions do count for a lot. In most cases the first impression will formulate the entire behavioral pattern towards the specific person. While the instinct and experience are important factors in the first impression analysis, without a few insights on how to properly interpret what you see and the signals you receive, such analysis is statistically only 50% accurate and representative of the truth.

We used the example of Einstein to display one side of the equation. There is also another side. It is almost a certainty that a person in a well-tailored suite, clean, cleanly shaven and with a well-tented appearance will attract a favorable behavioral pattern. Yet, it is also a statistical fact that the worst crimes have been perpetrated by well-dressed, well-mannered and well-articulated persons. Persons that have painstakingly saw to it that absolutely no warning signals were sent before they completed their criminal activity.

It is very unusual, not to mention impossible, to be scammed by a badly dressed person. You may wrongly feel pity and help one, but they very rarely will cheat you out of everything you have. On the other hand, a well-dressed and well-versed investment analyst can leave you completely penniless and at the mercy of welfare and handouts. Especially if they used their power of persuasion to make you sign a power of attorney in their favor.

Many people wonder how it is possible to distinguish the true character traits of a person they see for the first time. Especially when they have taken the time to train themselves in the art of deception. This is what this book is for. There are many ways to determine these traits and be right about it. There are also ways to cut through the deception and see what really lies underneath.

In the following chapters we will be talking about the eyes, the body language and the other signals that are emitted by all of us at all times. No matter how well trained a person is, some of these signals cannot be masqued. And for those that are masqued it is just a matter of identifying the error. Because there will always be an error. It doesn't have to be an error in the setup. It may just be that the feeling radiating from the person is one of a makeshift behavioral pattern.

This kind of assessment would be especially beneficial in the case of politicians. In fact their behavioral patterns have frequently been explored in the science of micro-expression analysis. Since the general public does not have access to this kind of technology it would be very useful to learn a few techniques to identify the truth from the lies that politicians always serve. This way we could reasonably vote for the best of them.

Such analysis is also very useful in situations where we are about to enter into a business relationship. Business relationships are about money and profit. And they are ruthless so there is very little room for mistakes in the initial impression analysis. Such mistakes will cost a lot of money, even lead us out of the business altogether.

It would be useless to go into details on how the first impression and the infatuation that results can lead us to huge mistakes in personal relationships. Just imagine how many marriages and how many friendships would have taken a different turn if the people involved were able to correctly judge who they were dealing with. And since it is usually these relationships that usually draw out the worst parts of our characters when they go south, think of how many of them would not have resulted in killings, beatings, abuses and suicides.

Under this perspective, it is actually an imperative to learn how to properly size up a person. While a society without feelings may not be the ideal one, a society that can limit the reactions to these feelings to just fights, bad words and crimes of indiscretion is infinitely better than a society full of guns, ammo and dead bodies.

It all starts with the eyes. Very little of a person's character can be covered if there is proper interpretation of the messages and signals the eyes send. And this is the subject of the next chapter.

THE EYES

We all know that the eyes are the mirror of the soul. They reflect the feelings of the moment, the thoughts behind the words and the clarity or blackness of the inner makings of a person. The eyes tell the truth about the visionary, the idealist and the artist. They also give away the dishonest, the cheater and the one that promises to bash your head open having the stone already inside their pocket.

The story the eyes tell begins with the eye color. People with eyes darkly colored tend to be more dominant in any sort of relationship, have more powerful personalities, tend to be better at sports and are generally considered as most trustworthy. On the other hand people with lighter colored eyes can handle more pain, are sort of bitchy and are considered to be sexier.

People with brown eyes are considered as more responsible, friendlier, mostly serious but at the same time as people that can live a little, have some fun and be practical. Blue eyes are a completely different story. They can be the most sincere in a gathering, with a bright and happy nature, they are highly intellectual but they can also be as cold and heartless as a stone.

Green eyes are considered as mysterious. People with green eyes can be unpredictable, they love freedom and independence and they are considered as performing better under pressure. They project a great amount of sex appeal and, as this is a predominant influence, they can easily be underestimated as far as the rest of their qualities and character traits are concerned. Consequently they can be considered as untrustworthy. However this is a deduction that will come after an unfortunate fact.

The color is only the first step and you should not base your analysis on that alone. Too many people wear contact lenses that change their eye color. If your own eyesight is strong enough to detect the lenses you can proceed to the next step with full awareness, otherwise you should do so by keeping such a concept in your mind.

A definite indication of lying is a response that is accompanied by darting or shifting of the eyes. Those are also indications of thinking about alternative answers to a question. Alternatives that can have the least damaging consequences but that will also not be true. The same deduction is most usually the case when the direction of the stare is downwards. This usually indicates guilt or shame about a response that the person giving it knows that it is a lie.

Of even more significance is a stare that is directed upwards and to the left. This indicates that the person is making up the response. Many people misunderstand the stare as an attempt to remember a visual experience. This is the case when the direction of the stare is directed only to the left and not upwards. Similarly a stare directed to the right, is an attempt to remember an auditory experience. A stare right and upwards indicate a dishonest reconstruction of events.

An unfocused stare directed upwards, forwards or downwards indicates that the person accompanies and supports their words with images in their minds. Similarly if the direction of the unfocused stare is in the direction of the ears, it means that the person is supporting their speech with sounds. A person sticking their stare downwards supports what they say with feelings. The difference pertaining to the sincerity of what is said is the unfocused stare with eyes that remain open while the gaze is intense.

The greatest misunderstandings occur with persons that look directly in the eyes. This is not a sign of sincerity as most people believe. It actually means insecurity as the person gazing at you this way does so because they want to gauge your reactions and adopt their behavior accordingly. Direct eye stare also means that the person is very submissive.

A person actively seeking persistent direct eye contact is also a person trying to gain dominance and intimidate the other side of the conversation and win an argument. This kind of behavior indicates a person that wants to make the others feel that they are superior and that they can do what they want with them. It puts people on the defensive and some of them may react exactly as required. Submit to the will of the person in active pursuit of persistent eye contact. However, some may not react this way and the outcome may be rather unfortunate.

Here comes the first exception to this rule. Under no circumstances is anyone to seek active direct eye contact with a person coming from Japan. It is considered disrespectful and a cause for discourse.

In the ways that separate the truth from deception as far as the eyes are concerned, is the ability to monitor the pupils. People have no control over their pupils. When they are dilated it means that they are interested either in a person or for the topic of the conversation. Dilated pupils also mean sincerity especially in emotional outbreaks.

Contracted pupils on the other hand indicate dishonesty and a lack of interest either in the person at the other side of the conversation or in the general proceedings of the moment. Make sure that when you make the observation you account for the presence or not of bright light. Regardless of the emotion, bright lights always contract the pupils.

All the above are results of studies conducted specifically for the purpose of analyzing a person. As aforementioned they are not infallible. They can be correct for the vast majority of the cases in question but not all of them. Plus there are some more issues to address when it comes to the signals sent by the eyes.

The most important issue to consider is the possibility of an eye condition of the person in question. People suffering from a number of medical conditions will avoid eye contact because their eyes cannot handle it. Consequently they can get misunderstood and misanalysed. A similar situation occurs to people suffering from sensitivity to light.

Other issues will come up from cultural and racial imperatives. This is actually an issue that pertains to all kinds of analysis for a person. People with different cultural backgrounds judge a person differently and act differently. This is why to the analysis of the eyes, additional observations are required. Let's begin with the discussion about what you hear in the next chapter.

WHAT YOU HEAR

While the observation of the eyes does not require any special technique other than the presence of mind, to analyze a person based on their speech and articulation patterns does require a small trick. You need to keep the topic of the conversation within or around a subject that is of common interest. This will allow the person you need to observe to speak more, elaborate more and loosen up more. All you need to do is sit back and listen. Carefully.

The presence of mind is still required because sometimes you need to read between the lines and make assumptions based on the context. Not everyone is able to articulate their thoughts and their meanings in a way that every listener can understand. And not everyone can have the communication skills to articulate what they say properly.

The level of education is clearly displayed by a well-spoken person. As is the level of knowledge about the topic of the conversation. The more one knows about a subject, the less they talk. And when they talk what they say is short, to the point and leaving no margin for errors or misunderstandings. Sometimes these people are annoyed if they are asked to elaborate more, or explain their terms as they expect you to know what they are talking about in advance.

However, the true personality is not revealed in a high level conversation. It is revealed in small talk. High level conversations very rarely allow for humor or for innuendo and evasion. Small talk is what allows for the display of the humorous side of a person as well as their response readiness and their wits.

Surprisingly the higher the level of education is the less these people are inclined to engage in small talk. They find the concept annoying and disruptive of their train of thought. It is a very frequent phenomenon that they may engage in a conversation as long as it pertains to a topic that holds their interest. As soon as it drifts to small talk, they withdraw from the conversation and remain silent until another topic arises that is also of interest.

People of a lower level of education show fear in engaging to a conversation even if it is just small talk. They are afraid that their shortcoming will become obvious and they do not engage unless addressed to directly. And then they respond with very short sentences that very often contain the meaning "I have no idea what you are talking about." Especially if a person involved in the conversation is one that commands their respect.

All of the above are also indicative of the aggressiveness of a person's character. An aggressive character will participate in any level of conversation without caring if they are characterized as ignorant and annoying. Aggressive characters do not care about knowledge. They care about making their presence known and they are looking to assert their dominance especially when a conversation involves more than one person. They do so by diverting the topics to subjects they know about or by verbally abusing people, or by chastising the participants on their choice of topic by indicating that "it is not the place or the time to discuss such things."

However, those are not the only ones who may engage in any level of conversation. People that want to learn also do so but through a totally different approach. They ask questions. Carefully phrased questions that intend to invoke answers that will satisfy their ignorance. They are easily recognized by the others, but they are also respected as they have the awareness to know that their level of knowledge is low and they want to enhance it, contrary to the aggressive characters who are more or less despised of.

No matter what the level of conversation is there are two definite ways to identify a deception attempt. First of all the voice of the speaker changes. The pitch and the intonation become distinctly different than usual and the rhythm of the speech slows down. However, since these are also indications that there may be a perfectly plausible response to the situation that is not readily available, the second part is the crucial one in identifying the lie.

It is actually a very delicate point and it requires close attention. The process begins with an attempt to repeat a question or a statement. The delicate point is the tone of the voice and the choice of words.

A positive or almost angry "what's that supposed to mean?" or "come again?" or "excuse me?" or "run that by me again?" indicates that there may have been a misunderstanding of the original statement and a clarification is required before a response. They also indicate that the original statement or question may have offended the person under observation and it is their way of giving a chance to revise the offensive part before they respond appropriately.

On the other hand if the tone becomes doubtful and hesitant and the words used amount to "could you please say that again" it is a definite signal that "I heard you the first time and I am trying to buy time to find a response that will bring out the least of any negative consequences." This response will be evasive, diverting, even a direct lie. In any case it will not be a straight forward and true one.

The eyes and the speech are half the equation needed in the correct initial analysis of a person. Both are mostly true but they are also not infallible. This is why even more steps are required. Let's move on to step number three which is the total body language. If one has mastered the art of concealing the first two steps it is difficult to conceal this one too.

The Body Language

A few years back people did not even take notice on what someone's body was saying. Politicians are those that made it necessary to start thinking about the body language and the irrevocable indications of their lying. As the research went deeper and deeper into this subject the body language changed name. It is now called "non-verbal communication". The numbers are staggering.

Only 7% of what we communicate to another person comes from speech. 38% comes from what is called paraverbal communication and has to do with the inflection and the volume of the voice and 55% comes from the facial expressions, the posture, the attitude and the gestures we make.

As the researchers put it, paraverbal and non-verbal communication does not lie. They are supported by the limbic brain instead of the neocortex and the body knows what the truth is. So it expresses it regardless of what we do or think as if it has no other option. However, it is important to place every situation in its proper context otherwise the analysis will be completely off.

For example, if in a normal conversation there is a declaration that "I will say this only once" it is usually followed by a lie. But, if we are talking about a parent talking to their child or an officer talking to a subordinate it means that what follows is a statement that MUST be followed (an order in the case of the military) or there will be consequences.

If an answer to the question is yes and the person raises their shoulders, their response is that they do not know. Similarly if a person moves the head to one side and then the other, their answer is NO. However, teachers may go through the same gestures, only in pretense that they do not know the answer, in order to force their students to come up with the correct answer.

An analysis of a person through body language without the proper context and without knowledge of details such as medical conditions, autism, Asperger's syndrome and nervous ticks will actually end up being completely wrong and the conclusions derived will be inaccurate.

There are 4 categories of body language that should be considered:

FACIAL EXPRESSIONS

Facial expressions are the easier to analyze as it is easier to observe when you talk to someone. Mostly they are observed to indicate lies and dishonesty. For example:

a) A smile that extends only to the corner of the mouth is fake. A true smile creates wrinkles at the corner of the eyes.

b) A truth that has been told creates a symmetry in the facial expression. A lie on the other hand creates an asymmetry.

c) Watching over glasses is just a gesture of convenience. It does not mean criticism or spying.

d) Any intense state involves wetting of the eyes, a moisty nose and swallowing of saliva. Any of the three missing means that the emotion is not true but simulated.

HANDS TO HEAD

Every gesture of one or both hands to the head has a significance. This is one of the things that people who train themselves to deception take exceptional care for. If you see a person that makes absolutely no gesture with the hands against the head, it means that they have been intensely trained to do so. Let's discuss why:

If a person covers their mouth while speaking they are speaking lies. If they do that when the other person is speaking then they are skeptical to what they listen to, to say the least. In some interpretations this gesture means that the listener does not believe a word said. Covering of the mouth when no one is speaking accompanied with an "hmmm..." and uncovering it before any sentence is articulated means that there was considerable thinking before a response.

In this case what matters is the context. It would be natural to fully consider a response to a technical or scientific question, or in general a question that would require careful deliberation before answering. In any other case it means that the response may not be complete, sincere and to the point.

a) Placing glasses or a pen in the mouth, if it is not a nervous tick, means uncertainty.

b) A hand stretching of the earlobe or a finger inside the collar indicates uncertainty about what is being said and that something is held back in the conversation. A lie of omission is still a lie.

c) Rubbing of the chin or a thumb under the cheek indicate that the listener completely disagrees with what is being said.

d) An ear pushed forward means "stop talking. I'm not listening anymore and I have something to say."

e) Hand to the forehead

This one is really tough if there is no knowledge about an incident that may have preceded the conversation. In general it means shame, embarrassment and an attempt to hide. However, if there has been a previous situation were a serious problem has been divulged, it means that the person is not paying attention to the conversation, has the problem in their minds and is trying to find a solution to it.

What makes the difference is the positioning of the elbow. If it is placed inside the body it denotes its general meaning. If it is positioned outside it is an indication of a problem.

HANDS TO BODY

Some of the gestures that the hands make against the body can be trained. In fact in some situations there is intense training involved and not for the purpose of deception.

HANDS BEHIND THE BACK

Accompanied by the chest leaning forward and the chin being up indicate authority. They also indicate courage. All officers are trained to assume this posture in front of their men to inspire confidence in their ability to lead and submission to their orders.

This is true as long as one hand is holding the other by the wrist. If the hands are held in the forearms it actually indicates insecurity, fear and mistrust.

HANDS IN FRONT HELD BY THE FOREARMS

In general this has the same meaning as the arms in the back held in the same way. However, they may also indicate anger especially if accompanied by a leaning of the upper part of the body backwards and tilting of the head to a side. A very slight difference to observe is that in the second case, only the dominant hand is holding the other by the forearm. The weak hand is clinched in a fist and is hidden underneath the forearm of the dominant hand.

HANDSHAKES

Asymmetrical handshakes indicate approachability and friendliness. Slow handshakes indicate safety, security and patience. The also indicate people that know that they have something important to say and all the time in the world at their disposal to say it.

a) Folded hands are the worst kind of message. The message received is blocked, the person talking is a complete stranger, everything is a matter of skepticism and not to be taken at face value, there is a lot of negativity and the person always assumes a defensive position not open to any suggestions unless there is ample and undeniable proof attached. Even so it may take a second opinion to loosen up and abandon the defensive position.

b) Thumbs inside the pockets with the rest of the hand outside, or thumbs outside the pockets with the rest of the hand inside, indicate strength, domination and sexual aggressiveness.

c) Attempts to clean nonexistent lint from clothing indicate that the person disapproves of what is being said but is unable to come up with convincing contradictive arguments.

d) Playing with non-cylindrical objects indicates awkwardness. Playing with cylindrical objects, especially for the ladies, indicates courtship.

POSITION OF THE FEET

This is usually a part that behavioral training may forget. Yet, the position of the feet in a conversation can be very important.

a) The usual positioning of the legs one above the other indicates that the person that stands in the direction pointed by the knee that is on top is of more interest. Behavioral training on this takes extra special care in the top knee pointing nowhere.

b) Talking to a person with the legs pointed in a different direction is a strong indicator that the conversation is to end so that you can move to the direction your legs are pointing.

c) If the legs and the hands are crossed in a sitting position it means that the person is withdrawn from the conversation. The same kind of crossing in a standing position means that the people discussing are unknown to each other.

d) Supporting the body on one leg and having the other one pointed to the direction of an individual means that you consider this individual to be the most important part of the conversation.

It is obvious that the body language has too many aspects to observe and it may take some time and effort from the observer's part to practice observing all of them so that a safe conclusion can be derived. However, there is one more point to be discussed that has to do with the correct initial analysis of a person. The point of the outward appearance which is discussed in the next chapter.

THE OUTWARD APPEARANCE

This is the part that has been the point of debate for thousands of years. The point that many wise people in the past have tried to persuade us that it is wrong to judge someone just by the way they look. A certain story of a person called Jean Valjean comes to mind… Too many people have been abused in the past just because they looked like criminals. Too many people have been executed or left to rot in a dungeon for the same reason.

It definitely is a mistake to base an analysis solely on what you see the first time you meet someone. If you meet them at all and not turn away to leave immediately. There have been many documented cases of such reactions even nowadays when supposedly people are more educated and should know better than to react this way. However, it is another irrefutable fact that pacifists may not even want to talk to a person that belongs to a police or military organization, Christians may turn away and leave at the site of a Muslim and Caucasians may forbid the participation to a conversation of an African without even waiting to meet the person in question who may have something to contribute.

Yet, it remains an undeniable fact that the very first impression and the very first conclusion is immediately drawn upon the first glance. Even before any proper introductions. It is in the natural order of things and it is useless to deny it. The only thing that can be said on the subject is to at least have the courtesy to extend to this person the benefit of the doubt.

The most usual mistake made is by men judging the first glimpse they get of a woman. Women have the habit of paying very close attention to their appearance when they go out to meet people or even go to work. A sexy appearance always induces sexual comments and conclusions that do not go any deeper. Yet, it is a very frequent phenomenon that it will not be long before men discover that the certain lady is not at all what they expected to say the least.

Similarly a fat lady or a woman that has not paid attention to her appearance may not even attract a second glance from men. Not to mention what happens if they try to join a conversation where they are simply ignored unless they are called to join by a common friend.

If all the above were to be avoided and more careful observations made, it would be possible to learn a lot more about a person's character. For example someone (man or woman) that is first seen wearing gym clothes but not carrying a gym bag is a strong indication that they have a car nearby. By extension, carrying a gym bag and wearing dirty running shoes, means that they have just finished running in a muddy terrain and they are on their way home.

Big sized men with long beards always insight feelings of fear and put the others on the defensive no matter what they wear. However, a closer look may indicate that the beard is well tended and the clothes are clean and ironed and therefore the person has someone taking care of him and is sociable. On the other hand untended beards, wrinkled clothing and old shoes indicate that this person is living alone and may have reduced social skills.

Better assumptions on a personality can be derived from the way they walk. A person that walks with wide steps is a person full of confidence on their own abilities. It is also a courageous person that has no problem to lead. A person that walks heavily does not mean that they are fat. It means that they are very persistent and probably stubborn to the point of inflexibility. Someone that walks slowly and by dragging the feet has no energy and is probably on the verge of depression.

Cat walking is a show off unless someone has been specifically trained to do so after years of practice. The same stands true for those who walk as if they were models participating in a fashion show. In any case any person walking fast without a specific reason that indicates they are in a hurry, is a person that is in a good mood. Especially if the head looks high at the same time. Similarly a person walking slowly (without dragging the feet) and with the head looking down to the ground is in a very bad mood and probably in a lot of personal or professional trouble. Especially if they keep the hands in their pockets and accompany their walking by talking to themselves.

Very few other than the aforementioned conclusions can really be derived out of the outward appearance. It's not only that in most cases there is no knowledge of where a person has been and what they were doing before we had the first glance of him. It is also a matter of cultural imperatives and differences. Some appearances that may look strange to Americans may be absolutely normal for people from Europe. Arabs have completely different sets of criteria than Asians.

Outward appearance is the wrong way to derive final conclusions. Not without at least allowing for the person to be introduced and exchange a decent discussion. A lot more will be derived from the posture, the body language, the eyes and the voice than the clothes worn or the condition of general cleanliness. It is natural to analyze a person at first sight. It is natural to derive conclusions at first sight. But most of the times those are the wrong conclusions. You need to combine the total set of observations before finalizing the analysis. At that point the observations filtered through the knowledge, instinct and experience will draw the right conclusion.

CONCLUSION

We see a person for the first time. Immediately an opinion is formed. It doesn't matter if it is positive or negative. Every interaction with this person after that will be based on this initial opinion which may very well be wrong. It is this first opinion that has resulted in countless crimes in the past. Unjustifiable crimes that drew out the need to form ways to analyze people that are correct and based on scientific findings.

At first people began analyzing the eyes. The notion that they are the mirrors of the soul and that not many things can be hidden led to a few ways to observe how the eyes behave and incorporate the results of the observation to the initial opinion. However, dishonesty and the need to cheat for profit led to ways that people overcame these ways. Not to mention that not everyone was offered access to the knowledge of how to properly read eyes.

The next step was to introduce the analysis of the verbal communication skills. How well the sentences are articulated, the tone of the voice, the pitch, the intonation and what to observe to spot the lies. For most people the research behind this sort of analysis still remained undisclosed and they relied heavily on their instinct and experience into sorting out the truth.

Which became even more useful when it was discovered that people trained themselves to get over this analysis and still be able to cheat.

Finally it was made clear that more than half of the messages that were emitted by a person during a conversation were coming from their body. Initially it was described as body language and then it was dubbed as "non-verbal communication". Gradually all this knowledge is coming out in the open so that more and more people can derive the correct conclusions and distinguish the truth from any attempts for cheating.

With all of the above been said there is an element that must always be kept in mind when it is time to draw our final conclusions. The context of the entire process. The benefit of the doubt must be extended even after all the observations have been gathered and interpreted. It is not always known if there are extenuating circumstances behind this first meeting that can skew the results or if there are any other aspects that should be taken into account like medical conditions and disorders.

This context must also be extended to people from different cultures and different religious and ideological backgrounds. It is in our nature to form the first opinion. It is also in our nature to base everything on this first opinion. Knowledge and observation will modify this first opinion. Until all of the circumstances are fully known we must always keep in mind that they are mostly correct. Not infallible.

www.ingramcontent.com/pod-product-compliance
Lightning Source LLC
Chambersburg PA
CBHW070240290526
45789CB00004B/1703